The Crafter's Design Library

Fantasy

Chris Down

David & Charles

A DAVID & CHARLES BOOK

First published in the UK in 2004

Distributed in North America
by F&W Publications, Inc.
4700 E. Galbraith Rd.
Cincinnati, OH 45236
1-800-289-0963

ISBN 0 7153 1579 X hardback
ISBN 0 7153 1580 3 paperback (USA only)

Printed in Singapore by KHL
for David & Charles
Brunel House, Newton Abbot, Devon

commissioning editor Fiona Eaton
desk editor Jennifer Proverbs
executive art editor Ali Myer
book designer Lisa Forrester
production controller Jennifer Campbell
crafter Cheryl Owen
photographer Ginette Chapman

Visit our website at www.davidandcharles.co.uk

David & Charles books are available from all good bookshops; alternatively you can contact our Orderline
on (0)1626 334555 or write to us at FREEPOST EX2 110, David & Charles Direct, Newton Abbot, TQ12 4ZZ
(no stamp required UK mainland).

contents

the essential techniques

the templates

Introducing *Fantasy* art

Fantasy art provides a wealth of inspiration for the creative crafter, and the many designs and motifs collected in this book can be applied and adapted to the complete range of craft skills. Fantasy art designs are drawn from myths and legends, epic tales and romantic poems, ancient history and fantasy fiction.

The world of fantasy art is limitless – the restrictions are merely those of the imagination. Yet at the same time, fantasy art is rooted in the experience and observation of the very world it seeks to go beyond. Images are at once strange and familiar. A Pegasus is formed from horses and birds, its existence an amalgamation of the two. A castle may be created using established building principles then exaggerated. A warrior may have weapons and armour adapted from different eras. The beauty of this is there are no fixed rules. No detail can be said to be wrong, as it is all pure imagination. This allows the artist immense freedom.

Ancient art

From the earliest cave paintings, humanity has attempted to reflect the world around it. Yet right from the beginning, alongside familiar creatures such as horses, reindeer and bison were fantastic beasts drawn from the dark fears and vivid imaginations of the artists. As civilizations developed, so did their mythologies and pantheons of gods and goddesses who could take on many shapes and forms.

Most early art is associated with religion, as materials and surfaces on which to place art were precious and scarce, and these ancient images are often sources of inspiration for fantasy art today. From the deities of Ancient Egypt with animal heads attached to human bodies depicted on the walls of the pyramids, to the fabled Chinese dragon and the grotesque gargoyles adorning the walls of Gothic churches and cathedrals across Europe, all cultures have created fantastical creatures.

Fantasy art and literature

Fantasy fiction and fantasy art have evolved together. Fantasy fiction ranges from children's literature that draws on old folklore and mythologies packed with tales of dragons, fairies, mermaids and goblins to the many romantic and heroic tales for the adult market. These books have provided a major outlet for the fantasy art form, which is an extension of the knowledge and experiences of the authors, the observations and research of the artists.

This link between literature and art can be found in some of the work of the Pre-Raphaelite artists and symbolists of the late 19th century who often took the work of romantic poets such as Alfred Lord Tennyson as their inspiration. Sir Edward Burne-Jones for example, spanned both movements and embraced ideas familiar to the modern fantasy artist such as pseudo-medieval Arthurian romance.

If there is a defining moment in the development of the fantasy world, it has to be the publication of J.R.R. Tolkien's *The Lord of the Rings*. This one story, and the world it encompasses, contains so many elements of fantasy that decades after its appearance the appeal still endures.

It describes extraordinary creatures, races of flamboyant diversity, powerful magic, landscapes of mystery, a quest to save the world and an ancient land in a process of transition to another age.

Tolkien went further than most in the creation of his world, spending decades developing a vast mythology of races, languages and histories. He drew from his background and experiences to flesh out his story. Tolkien was a professor of Anglo-Saxon at Oxford University and his interest in the epic poem Beowulf as well as the influence of Norse mythologies resonate through *The Lord of the Rings*. He fought in the battle of the Somme, and the horrors of World War I are reflected in his fictional battle scenes.

The boom years

The cheaply produced pages of comic books and pulp fiction paperbacks that flourished in the early part of the 20th century can probably be considered the modern birthplace of fantasy art. Here, dreams of other worlds were allowed to take shape. Initially budgets and production standards were low, and the mass produced printing processes were raw. However, the genre proved popular and it began to grow, reaching a peak in the 1960s and 1970s as talented artists found an outlet for their skills producing more and more exciting results.

Science fiction art is often confused with fantasy art. There is a degree of overlap but a simple distinction can be made. Science fiction, as the name implies is more technology based and generally futuristic, involving space ships and ray guns. Fantasy tends towards the natural and pre-industrial, featuring unicorns and medieval knights.

Fantasy art in the 21st century

At the beginning of the 21st century, the outlets for fantasy art have expanded beyond comic books and novels. In the age of computer graphics and Hollywood blockbusters, artists are migrating to new media. Some, who cut their teeth on book covers, are now acting as designers on films, others on computer games. Their scope and vision becoming three-dimensional worlds that reach audiences of millions.

Through the endeavours of these artists, designers and other creative fans of this age-old style, the world of fantasy can become a temporary reality, and an enduring art form for everyone.

About the book

Reaching into the wide world of fantasy art, this book is packed with a diverse range of designs, from simple motifs to more complex images that will appeal to both the novice and the experienced craft worker. It is ideal for crafters, artists and others who wish to apply fantasy designs to their projects but find the creation of the designs from scratch too daunting. The motifs are divided into themed chapters covering popular aspects of fantasy art including striking dragon heads (pages 58–67) and silhouettes of dancing pixies (pages 26–35), to Excalibur rising mysteriously from the waters of the lake (page 107). Whatever your taste, chosen craft and ability, you will find something to suit you.

The front section offers practical advice on using the motifs, with ideas for particular crafts (see page 8) and tips on adapting the designs to suit individual needs (see pages 9-11). Applying Motifs to Craft Media (pages 14-19) shows you how to transfer motifs to a number of popular craft media, such as glass, mirrored glass, paper, card, and fabrics including cross stitch fabric. Finally, the Project Gallery (pages 20-23) provides plenty of ideas, tips and inspiration on using the designs to great effect. So whatever your craft, all the information, ideas and motifs are in this book, ready for you to create amazing fantasy art projects.

Ideas for crafting

Glass painting The distinctive lines of many of the fantasy images are ideal for glass painting, where paint is flowed within shapes drawn with glass painting outliner. Use on both glass and acetate (see page 23).

Painted crafts Fantasy designs are very atmospheric and can give a historical or romantic feel to a painted item. Apply to wooden furniture and accessories (see page 22), walls, metal ware and ceramics (see page 17).

Stamping Choose simple motifs for stamping. Cut the images from fine foam, then apply to any number of surfaces, such as greetings cards.

Stencilling Many of the motifs can be traced and cut from stencil board. It is also simple to adapt some motifs for stencilling by adding 'bridges' between the sections to hold the stencil together (see page 19).

Découpage The fine detail of fantasy designs are very effective for découpage. Embellish with coloured pens and pencils, or photocopy the image onto coloured paper. Seal the finished paper design with sanding sealer on both sides, stick to your chosen surface with PVA (white) glue, then apply at least five coats of varnish.

Embossed metal Fine metals are available from craft shops in gold, aluminium, copper and bronze, and the design can be embossed on their surface, then painted if you wish (see pages 15 and 20). Armoury motifs particularly lend themselves to this technique, and the images can be cut out and glued to boxes, greeting cards or made into jewellery.

Paper cuts Cut the splendid silhouettes of fairies, witches and castles that appear throughout the book from black paper and use to create pictures and greetings cards.

Candles Appliqué wax (a thin layer of candle wax on a paper backing) is available from craft shops and candlemaking suppliers. Cut a motif from the wax with a craft knife, carefully peel off the paper and press it onto a plain candle to make an impressive decoration (see page 23). Alternatively, use special candle paints to paint a design onto the candle.

Fabric painting Use fabric paint to embellish all kinds of fabrics. One technique is to photocopy your artwork onto Lazertran paper, then transfer the image onto materials such as T-shirts and cushions (see page 18).

Embroidery Work designs in colourful threads in a variety of stitches onto fabric (see pages 19 and 20). Alternatively, appliqué bold designs by hand or machine.

Silk painting Silk paints are flowed within outlines traced with silk outliner (gutta) onto silk that has been stretched on a silk frame. The designs can be made into luxurious scarves, evening bags and cushions.

Clay and salt dough modelling Use the fantasy motifs to model both flat designs for plaques and three-dimensional creations from clay (see page 21). Air-drying clay can be painted or left in its natural pale or terracotta finish, both of which would look great as castles. Polymer clay comes in lots of colours and is hardened in the oven. Use salt dough, made of plain flour, salt and water, to make flat designs, hardened in the oven.

Adapting and embellishing designs

There are many ways to use the templates from this book, depending on the craft and materials being worked. Here are some ideas for adapting and combining motifs to create unique designs appropriate to different types of projects. It may be necessary to simplify motifs for some craft work while others lend themselves to decorative detail, eye-catching backgrounds or the use of more than one image.

Simplifying a design

Most of the designs in this book are simple, without too many lines and details, to make them suitable for craft application. However, you may want them to be simpler still because of the limitations of the craft medium or because the image is to be used very small. The knight motif (see page 87) on the near right, is simplified by thickening the lines and removing rivets from the armour and decorative detail from the shield and the knight's chain-mail.

tip
Use a thick pencil, pen or outliner to transfer the simplified image to your craft project.

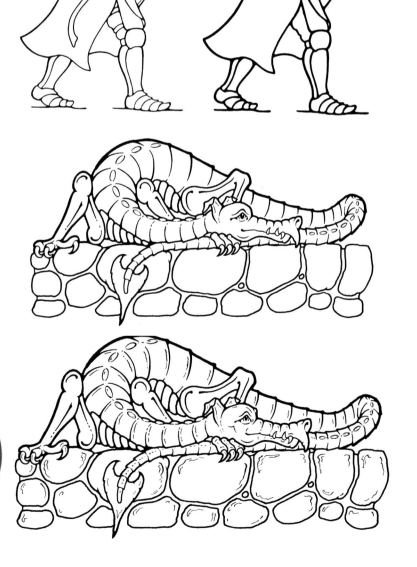

Adding detail to a design

If the craft project allows, you may wish to add detail to the design to create a more 'realistic' look. The dragon motif, top, (see page 64) has been developed by adding extra lines that give more information about the shape of the stones on the wall and the curve of the dragon's body. The larger a motif is used the more scope there is for adding detail, although the way in which it is to be applied also plays a key role.

tip
Trace off the motif and develop it with fine pencil before transferring to the craft project.

Combining templates

You can develop your own designs by combining different motifs, or just certain elements from motifs. The design, right, is created using a motif (page 29) from the Fairies, Elves and Pixies chapter, and a corner design from Borders and Backgrounds (page 119). Below is a design created from elements of the Horsemen and Heraldry chapter. You could also combine different themes – add a witch flying behind a castle or a knight battling a dragon.

tip
Experiment with resizing templates to make the combinations work for your project.

Creating a mirror image

Embellish a design by creating a mirror image of a motif and placing it in a border. For a seaside theme a mirror image mermaid (page 72) is placed inside a border made from shells (pages 72–73) – perfect for a bathroom stencil or mirror. Choose images in profile to mirror, such as a fairy, and place them in front of a single sun or moon outline.

tip
Trace off the different elements and create the final image required before you begin your project.

Adding borders

Use the border templates
(pages 114–119) to frame and
contain a motif and make a
self-contained design. This pixie,
right, (page 34) looks perfect in
the bluebell border (page 119)
and would make a fabulous plate
design. The Pisces motif (page 111)
looks wonderful within the stone effect border from
page 117. Make sure to match the motif with the
border design – animals and fairy creatures go well
with leaf borders, mythical creatures, wizards and
warriors sit nicely in Celtic or geometric designs.

tip

Motifs with flowing
lines suit circular
borders, while more
geometric designs sit
well in a square
surround.

tip

The more complex
the background, the
simpler the lines of
the motif need
to be.

Adding backgrounds

For craft work where lots of detail
is appropriate a background can
contain and show off a motif. This angel
(page 71) sits within an oval with a
fragmented background that creates a stained
glass effect. A mermaid could be nicely
mounted on a shell background or a fairy
backed by one large flower or a floral pattern.

Adding colour

There are many colour themes that could apply to fantasy art, and you are sure to gain inspiration from magazines, films and books. You will also find ideas in the subject matter you choose and in the projects you decide to make. There are no hard and fast rules, but here are some examples of colour applied to the motifs to get you started. Look throughout the whole front section to see more examples of colour being used to great effect.

Silhouettes

A quick and simple way to add colour and definition to a motif is to turn it into a silhouette, ideal for stamping and appliqué. Many of the motifs in this book have been designed for this purpose and would look striking against a coloured background. This pixie (page 30) looks lively and mischievous against the moonlit sky.

Harmonious tones

Colour does not always have to be bright or vibrant. This Viking ship scene (page 102) has been coloured in with harmonious sandy tones to give a warm, rich feel evocative of the pictures found in old books and manuscripts. Such a subtle effect would look stylish applied to a bag or T-shirt.

Shading and contours

This toadstool house (page 57) has been given subtle shading to highlight contours in the subject matter, such as the rounded walls and shadow under the roof. A whimsical feel is achieved through the use of bright, fresh colours. Such colours would also look charming applied to the fairies for a little girl's birthday card.

Bold contrasts

The use of contrasting colours, such as red and green, will help to make a motif stand out. The colours enhance each other and they really jump from the page to create an effect that is striking and bold. This mythical creature from page 70 appears to have flames sprouting from its wings, and the reds and oranges enhance this feature.

Colours of nature

Look to nature for inspiration – the ladybird (page 48) has naturally beautiful colourings and makes a pretty motif (see page 20). However, the image of the dragonfly (page 48) has been embellished with decorative colours and finishes by artists for many years, giving nature a helping hand and a fantasy feel to their crafts.

Applying motifs to craft media

The techniques used to apply your selected fantasy motif to a particular craft media will vary depending on the surface. The following pages offer some simple advice on how to do this for the most popular craft media. Guidance is also given on how to enlarge or reduce the motif to suit your requirements.

Enlarging and reducing a motif

You may want to alter the size of your chosen motif to suit your project. The size of the finished item will determine what line weight and level of detail is suitable (see pages 9–11 for tips). There are three ways to change the size of a motif:

using a photocopier

For fast and accurate results, use a photocopier to enlarge or reduce a motif. To do this, you need to calculate your enlargement percentage. First measure the width of the image you want to end up with. Here, the motif needs to be enlarged to 90mm (3½in). Then measure the width of the original motif, which in this case is 59mm (2⁵⁄₁₆in). Divide the first measurement by the second to find the percentage by which you need to enlarge the motif, in this instance 152%. Remember that an enlargement must always be be *more* than 100% and a reduction *less* than 100%.

If you wish to photocopy an image onto tracing paper, use tracing paper that is at least 90gsm in weight. When photocopying an image from tracing paper, place the tracing paper onto the glass, and then lay a sheet of white paper on top of it. This will help to produce a clear, sharp copy.

using a grid

If you do not have access to a photocopier, it is possible to enlarge or reduce a motif by hand, using a grid. To begin, use low-tack masking tape to secure a piece of tracing paper over the original design. Draw a square or rectangle onto the tracing paper, enclosing the image (see below). Use a ruler to divide up the square or rectangle in to rows of equally spaced vertical and horizontal lines. The spacing will depend upon the size and intricacy of the design. Complex designs should have lines about 1cm (⅜in) apart. Simpler ones can have lines 4cm (1½in) apart.

Now draw a square or rectangle to match your required design size, and draw a grid to correspond with the one you have just drawn over the image, as shown below. You can now begin to re-create the original image by redrawing it, square by square, at the required scale.

Transferring a motif

transferring a motif onto paper, card, wood, foam and foil

You may want to use a light box to trace an image directly onto a piece of paper or thin card. A light box is useful for tracing onto both paper and fabric, and is easy to improvize with household items. Balance a piece of clear plastic across a pile of books or furniture, and place a table lamp underneath. You are then ready to place your motif beneath paper, thin card and even some fabrics. However, this may not always be suitable for the medium you are working with, and so here is an alternative method.

First, trace the design onto tracing paper using a sharp pencil. Next, turn the tracing over and redraw on the wrong side with a soft lead pencil. Now turn the tracing over again, and use masking tape to secure it right side up onto your chosen surface. Carefully redraw the image – press firmly enough to transfer the motif, but take care not to damage the surface.

using a scanner

A third way to enlarge or reduce a motif is to scan the original image on a flatbed scanner. You can then either adjust the size using image manipulation software, or simply alter the percentage of your printout size. If the finished result is larger than the printer's capacity, some software will allow you to tile the image over several sheets of paper, which can then be joined together to form the whole image.

An image manipulation package may also allow you to alter the proportions of a motif, making it wider or narrower, for example. Take care not to distort it beyond recognition, though. Once you are happy with your image, it can be saved to be used again and again.

To emboss foil, simply take the original tracing and secure it to the foil surface, then rest the foil on some kitchen paper. Use an old ballpoint pen to press down on the tracing, embossing the metal below. Use the same technique on the back of the foil to produce a raised effect.

transferring a motif onto mirror and ceramic

Trace the motif onto tracing paper, then turn the tracing over and redraw on the wrong side using a chinagraph pencil. A chinagraph produces a waxy line that adheres well to shiny surfaces, which makes it ideal for transferring designs to coloured glass, mirrored glass and ceramic. Chinagraphs are prone to blunt quickly, but it doesn't matter if the lines are thick and heavy at this stage. Use masking tape to secure the tracing right side up onto the surface. Carefully redraw with a sharp pencil to transfer the image.

tracing a motif onto glass and acetate

Roughly cut out the motif and tape it to the underside of the acetate or glass with masking tape. It is helpful to rest glassware on a few sheets of kitchen towel for protection and to stop curved objects from rolling. The image will now show through the clear surface, and you can simply trace along the lines with glass outliner or paint directly onto the surface.

If you want to transfer an image onto opaque glass, or onto a container that is difficult to slip a motif behind, such as a bottle with a narrow neck, follow the instructions on page 15 for transferring a motif onto mirror or ceramic.

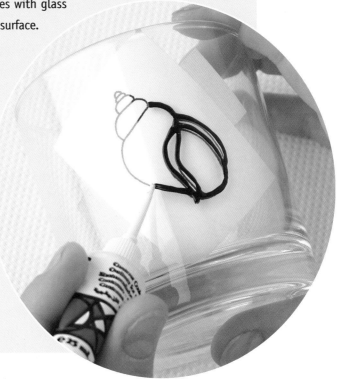

transferring a motif onto a double curvature

Motifs can be transferred onto rounded items, but will need to be adapted to fit the curves. First trace the motif, redrawing it on the underside (use a chinagraph pencil if the container is ceramic). Make cuts in the template from the edge towards the centre. Lay the motif against the surface so that the cuts slightly overlap or spread open, depending on whether the surface is convex or concave. Tape the motif in place with masking tape and transfer the design as before.

making a template for a straight sided container

If you wish to apply a continuous motif such as a border to a straight sided container, make a template of the container first. Slip a piece of tracing paper into a transparent glass container or around an opaque glass or ceramic container. Lay the paper smoothly against the surface and tape in place with masking tape. Mark the upper edge of the container with a pencil. Mark the position of the overlapping ends of the paper, or mark each side of the handle on a mug, cup or jug.

Remove the tracing and join the overlap marks, if you have made these. Measure down from the upper edge and mark the upper limit of the band on the template. Cut out the template and slip it into or around the container again to check the fit. Transfer your chosen template on to the tracing paper, then on to the container.

making a template for a plate

1 Cut a square of tracing paper slightly larger than the diameter of the plate. Make a straight cut from one edge to the centre of the paper. Place the paper centrally on the plate or saucer and tape one cut edge across the rim. Roughly cut out a circle from the centre of the paper to help it lie flat. Smooth the paper around the rim and tape in place, overlapping the cut edges. Mark the position of the overlap.

2 Turn the plate over and draw around the circumference onto the underside of the tracing paper. Remove the paper, then measure the depth of the plate rim and mark it on the paper by measuring in from the circumference. Join the marks with a curved line.

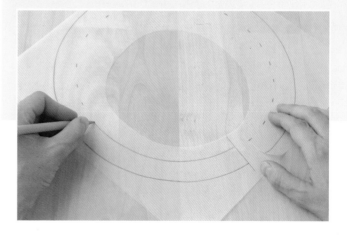

transferring a motif onto fabric

If the fabric is lightweight and pale in colour, it may be possible to trace the motif as it is. If the fabric is heavier, or a darker colour, it may help to use a light box. Place the motif under the fabric on the surface of the light box (see page 15 to construct a home light box). As the light shines up through the motif and fabric, you should be able to see and position the motif, ready for tracing.

Alternatively, place a piece of dressmaker's carbon paper face down on the fabric, as shown below. Tape the motif on top with masking tape. Trace the design with a sharp pencil to transfer it onto the fabric. The marks made by the carbon pencil are easily wiped away.

transferring a motif onto a knitting chart

Use knitting chart paper rather than ordinary graph paper to chart a knitting design (knitted stitches are wider than they are tall and knitting chart paper is sized accordingly). Transfer the motif straight onto the knitting graph paper (see page 15 for advice on transferring onto paper). Each square on the graph paper represents a stitch. Make sure that you are happy with the number of squares in the motif, as this dictates the number of stitches in your design, and ultimately the design size. Fill in the applicable squares on the chart using appropriate coloured pens or pencils.

Use the finished chart in conjunction with a knitting pattern. Read the chart from left to right for a knit row and from right to left for a purl row. The motif can also be worked on a ready knitted item with Swiss darning. Following the chart, work the first row from right to left and the next row from left to right.

transferring a motif onto needlepoint canvas and cross stitch fabric

Designs on needlepoint canvas and cross stitch fabric can be worked either by referring to the design on a chart, or by transferring the image to the canvas or fabric and stitching over it.

To transfer the motif onto a chart

Transfer the motif straight onto graph paper (see page 15 for advice on transferring onto paper). Each square on the graph paper represents a square of canvas mesh or Aida cross stitch fabric. Make sure that you are happy with the number of squares in the motif, as this dictates the number of stitches in your design, and ultimately the design size.

To transfer the motif directly onto canvas or fabric

An open weave canvas or light coloured fabric may allow you to trace the design onto the canvas or fabric. First, mark a small cross centrally on the motif and on the material. On a lightbox (see page 15), place the material on top of the motif, aligning the crosses. Tape in position and trace the image with a waterproof pen. Alternatively, dressmaker's carbon paper can be used to transfer a motif onto close weave canvas and cross stitch fabric (see opposite page for advice on transferring motifs onto fabric).

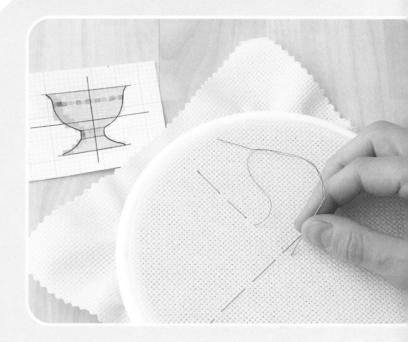

Colour in the squares that the motif lines cross with coloured pencils or pens. You may want to make half-stitches where the motif outline runs through a box. Mark the centre of the design along a vertical and horizontal line (see above). Run a line of tacking stitches on the needlepoint canvas or cross stitch fabric in the same way then work the stitches referring to the chart.

making a stencil

Tape a piece of tracing paper over the motif to be adapted into a stencil. Redraw the image, thickening the lines and creating 'bridges' between the sections to be cut out. You may find it helpful to shade in the areas to be cut out. Lay a piece of carbon paper, ink side down, on a stencil sheet, place the tracing on top right side up and tape in place. Redraw the design to transfer it to the stencil sheet then cut out the stencil with a craft knife, resting on a cutting mat.

Project gallery

embroidered napkin

This delicate image of a ladybird from page 48 works particularly well in its setting on a napkin subtlely printed with foliage. The insect was first transferred to the napkin with fabric carbon paper, then worked with three strands of stranded cotton (floss) embroidery thread in a variety of stitches including long and short stitch, satin stitch and French knots.

embossed watering can

The regal dragon emblem from page 61 is embossed onto metal with a ballpoint pen (a dried-up pen will do). The motif was traced onto tracing paper and taped face down onto a piece of fine copper metal. With the metal resting on a few sheets of kitchen towel, the image was redrawn with the pen to raise the outlines on the right side. The emblem was cut out and glued to a decorative watering can with all-purpose household glue. The subtle verdigris effect on the can was achieved by dabbing on three shades of aquamarine acrylic paint.

salt dough sun

It is hard to believe that this exotic sun face from page 109 is modelled from flour, salt and water. Eight tablespoons of plain flour were mixed with four tablespoons of salt. Four tablespoons of water were gradually added and kneaded to make a pliable dough. A 4cm (1½in) diameter ball of dough was flattened for the face. Sixteen 1.5cm (⅝in) diameter balls of dough were flattened slightly and squeezed to a point for the rays, then moistened and pressed around the face. A hole was pierced at the top for hanging. The sun was baked at 120ºC/250ºF/Gas Mark ½ for 5 hours, then painted with watercolour paints and varnished. Vibrant red cabouchon jewellery stones were glued on with strong epoxy resin glue as a finishing touch.

stencilled box

Stencilling is a very popular craft because it gives fast, professional results. This smart, pale blue wooden box has been stencilled with the magnificent beast from page 70 and edged with a border from page 119. The border is repeated on the sides of the box below a dramatic bat, from page 40. The images were transferred to stencil board and 'bridges' added to hold the designs together (see page 19). The images were then stencilled on with deep blue and purple acrylic paint and highlighted with silver paint.

appliquéd candle

Applique wax was used to create this mystical castle from page 91. The image was transferred onto the paper backing of the wax then cut out with a craft knife. The castle was then simply pressed in position on a coloured candle.

glass painted greetings card

Here, the cheeky pixie from page 27 has been traced with black glass outliner onto a sheet of acetate and then painted with glass paints and stuck with spray glue to white paper. A strip of coloured card was folded into three equal sections to make the greetings card. The outline of the painted image was traced onto tracing paper then used as a template to cut a window in the middle section, and the pixie glued behind the window. 5mm (¼in) was cut off the right hand section which was then glued behind the image.

the templates

Fairies, Elves and Pixies

Fairies and fairy-like creatures such as elves and pixies exist in many cultures around the world. They are renowned in legend and some people still believe in them. Time in the land of fairies passes so slowly that no-one ever dies, and a human who enters will be lost for years though they may believe they have only been gone for moments. Fairies come in all kinds of shapes, sizes and temperaments, although for the most part, they are thought of as small and elusive.

It seems that fairies have an ageless appeal: they have a magical allure for small children and yet the motifs here can be enjoyed by all lovers of fantasy, no matter what their age.

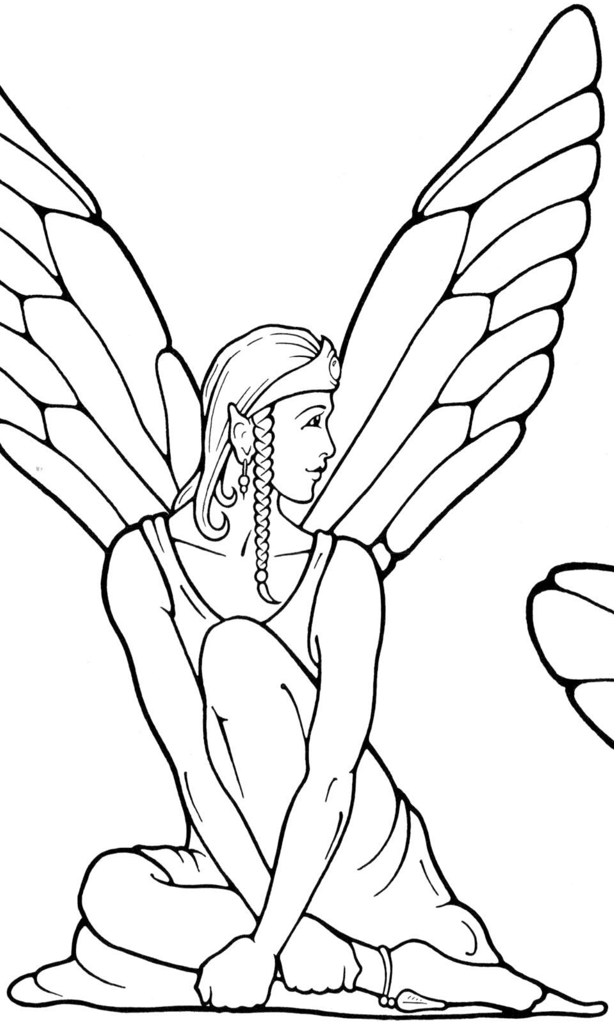

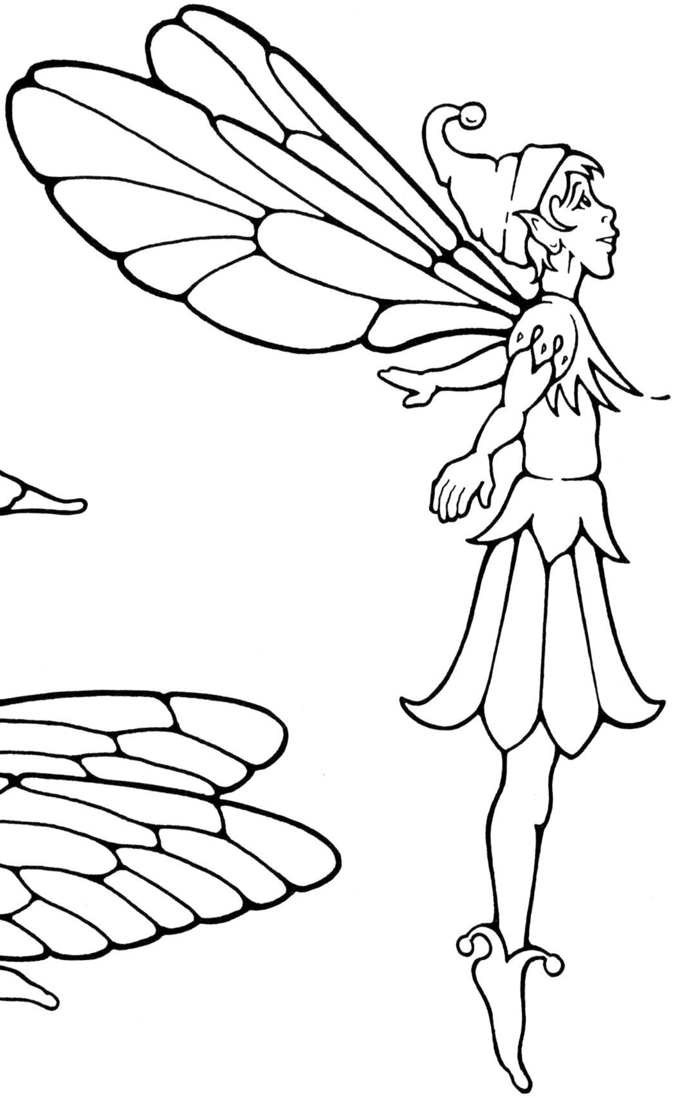

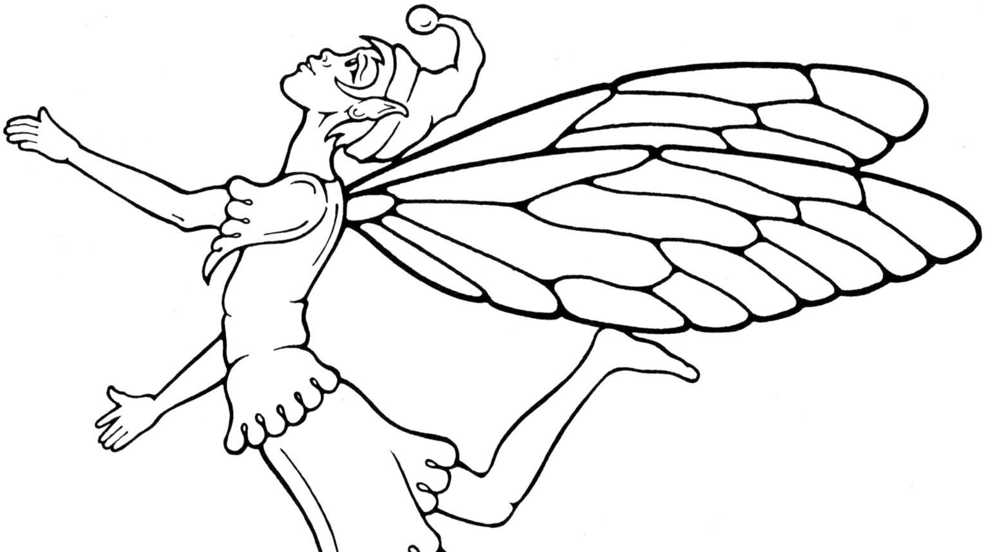

Witches and Wizards

For many centuries, witches had a bad press, and were often portrayed as wicked in stories such as *Snow White and the Seven Dwarfs*. Nowadays, witches and wizards can be the positive focus of fiction, even the hero of the day. Witness the rise of young wizard Harry Potter, a character popular with all ages, all over the world.

The motifs on these pages reflect the traditional halloween image of witches with pointy hats, black cats and broomsticks as well as the modern perception of witches as earth mothers, and wizards as wise men. These images will appeal to the many children keen on all things magical, as well as young people and adults interested in Wicca traditions.

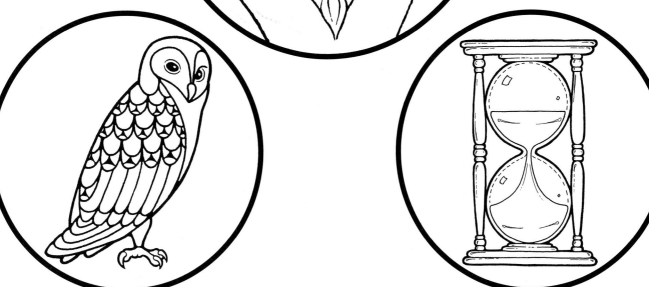

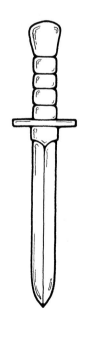

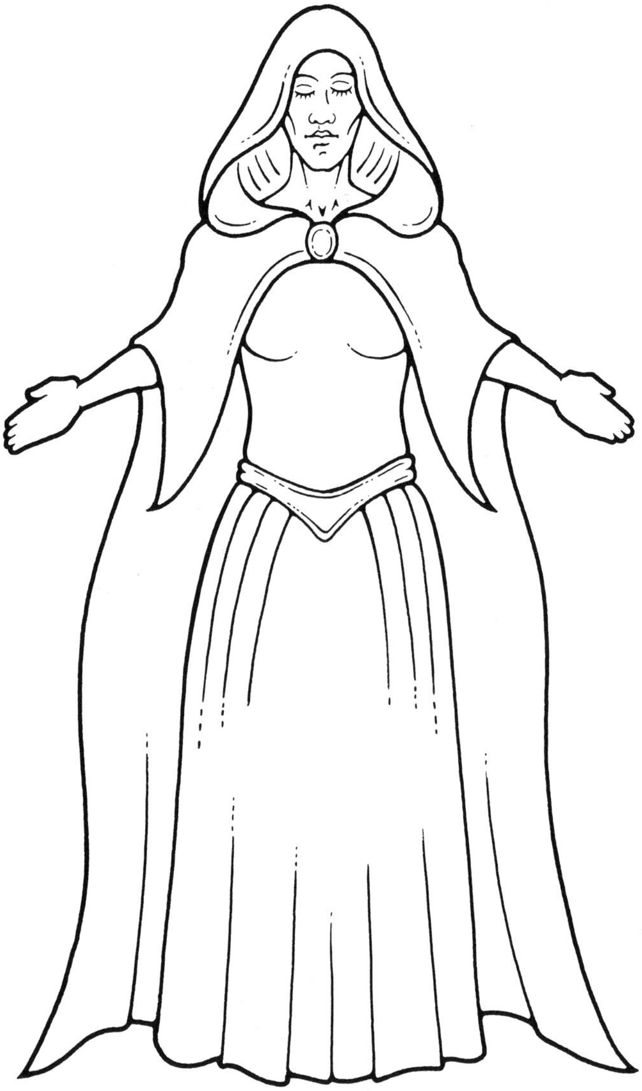

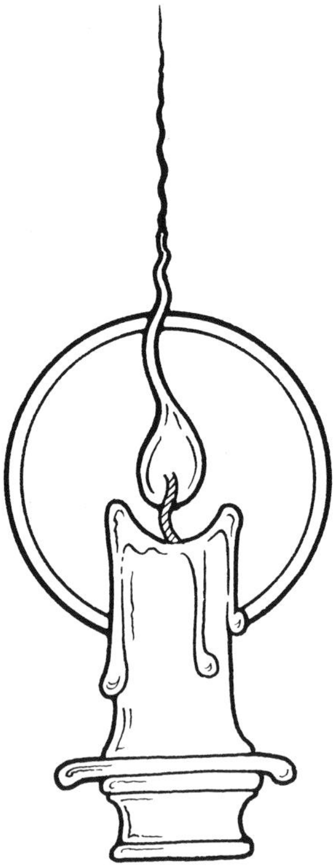

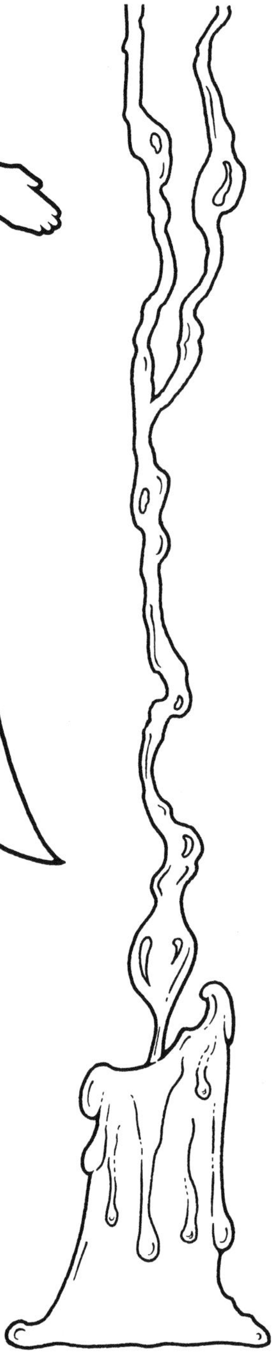

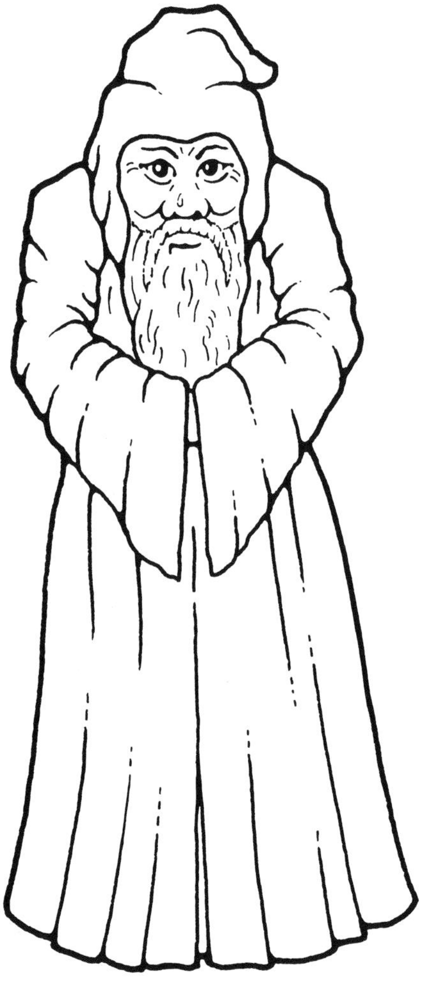

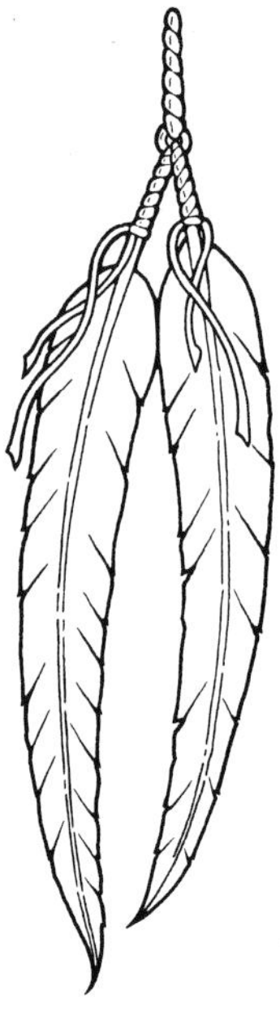

Glades and Grottos

A woodland glade or an underground grotto may be the home of fairies or trolls and goblins, or it may just be an image of the infinite mystery of the natural world.
The Green Man is a pre-Christian symbol of rebirth and regeneration. Christianity adopted its legend, and carvings of the Green Man can be found in many medieval churches. Today it has been embraced by those interested in ecological matters. In many cultures through history, trees are considered sacred and glades, in forests, the dwelling place of gods and spirits.

Forests are a haven for shy woodland creatures as well as even more reclusive fairy people, and the motifs in this section will also appeal to all those fond of the natural world, with its charming insect, animal and bird designs.

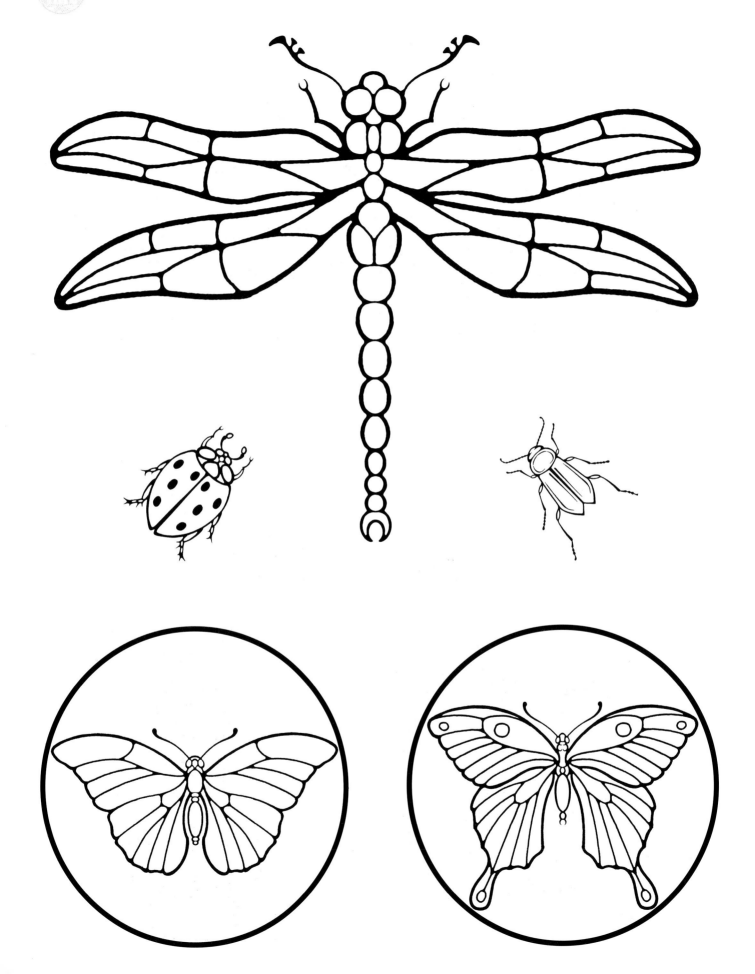

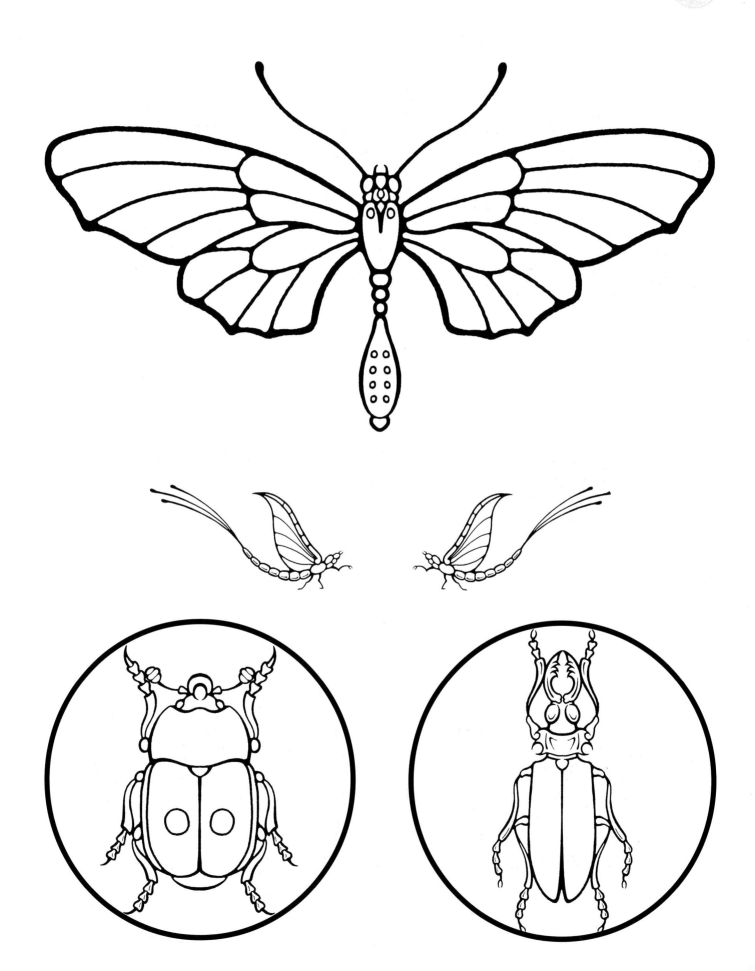

Dragons

The dragon features in the myths, legends and folklore of many European and Asian cultures. It is a powerful creature that commands both fear and respect. In western mythology it is a mighty and dangerous foe, providing the ultimate challenge for warriors of many heroic tales. In China, however, the dragon is considered to be a symbol of luck and a bearer of wealth.

Dragons have featured in stories for millennia: from the tale of the Greek and Roman god Apollo who slayed the dragon Python, to the Anglo-Saxon epic hero Beowulf who finally dies at the claws of a dragon. More recently the dragon Smaug plays a crucial role in J.R.R. Tolkien's fantasy story *The Hobbit*. Indeed, because it is so familiar, the dragon reigns supreme in the imagination of many as the ultimate creature of fantasy.

Mythical Beasts

A whole menagerie of spectacular creatures inhabits the world of myth, legend and the imagination. Many of these are combinations of two or more animals rather than entirely new creatures.

The addition of wings to a creature is a common way of creating a new, mythical beast. Pegasus is a horse with wings, and the griffin has an eagle's head and wings on a lion's body, while the hippogriff is a further combination of the griffin with a winged horse. The unicorn, a white horse with a horn, is the most romantic of the mythical creatures; considered both shy and elusive, it is swift and difficult to capture.

Horsemen and Heraldry

The classic fantasy warrior is often a knight drawn from the legend of King Arthur and his Knights of the Round Table. This story was written down in about 1150 by the Welsh chronicler, Geoffrey of Monmouth, and has been rewritten and added to many times since. Although Arthur was supposed to have reigned during the 500s, he and his followers are usually depicted as medieval knights in full armour, following the medieval code of chivalry – defending the church and protecting the weak.

The Arthurian legend has inspired artists, such as the Pre-Raphaelites, as well as writers and still captures the imagination of young and old alike. As with the best fantasy imagery, the motifs given here are created using a mixture of reality and imagination.

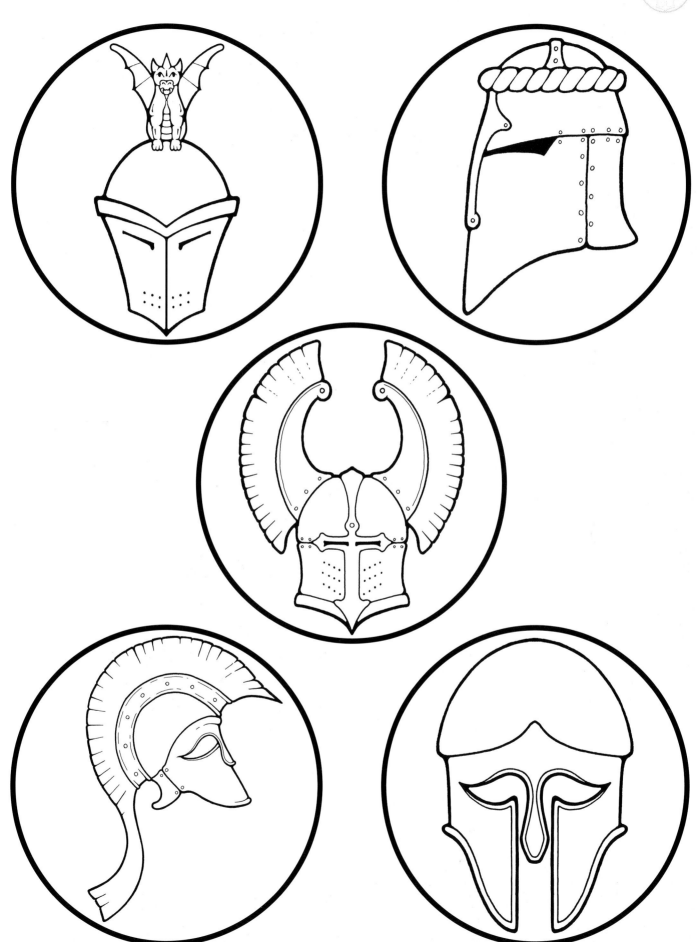

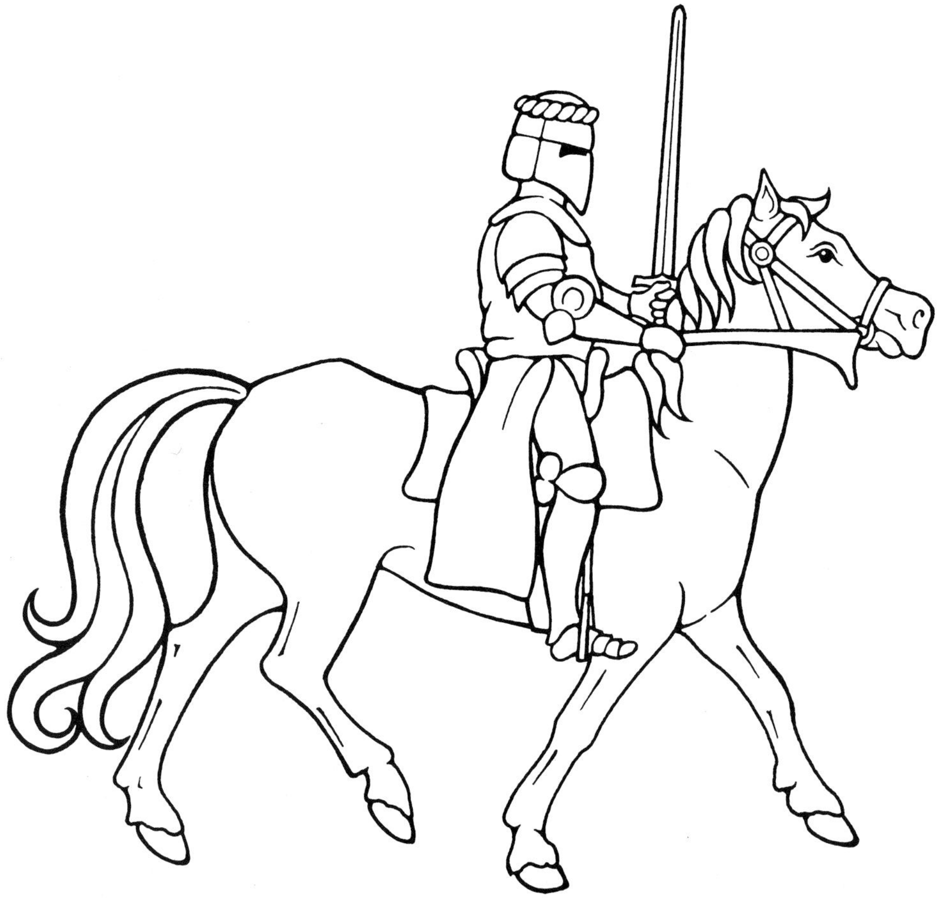

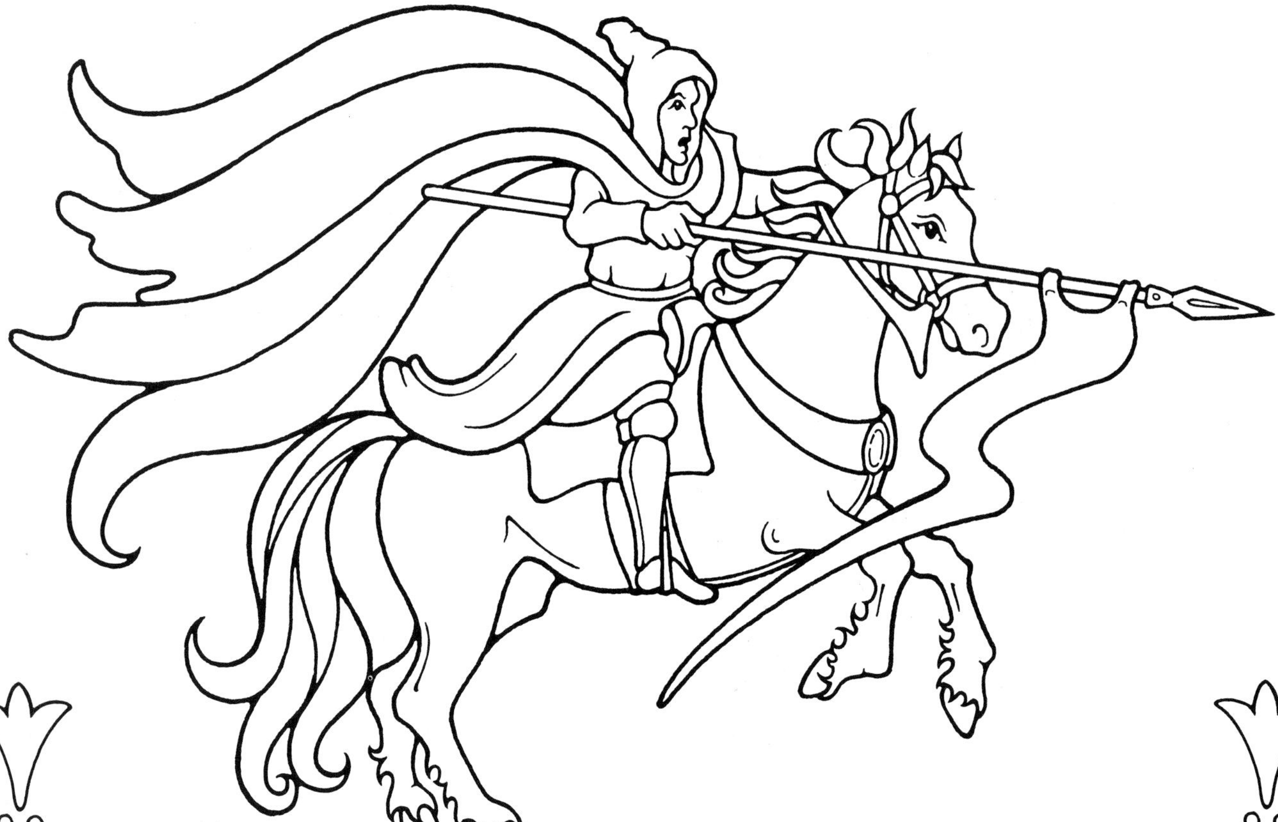

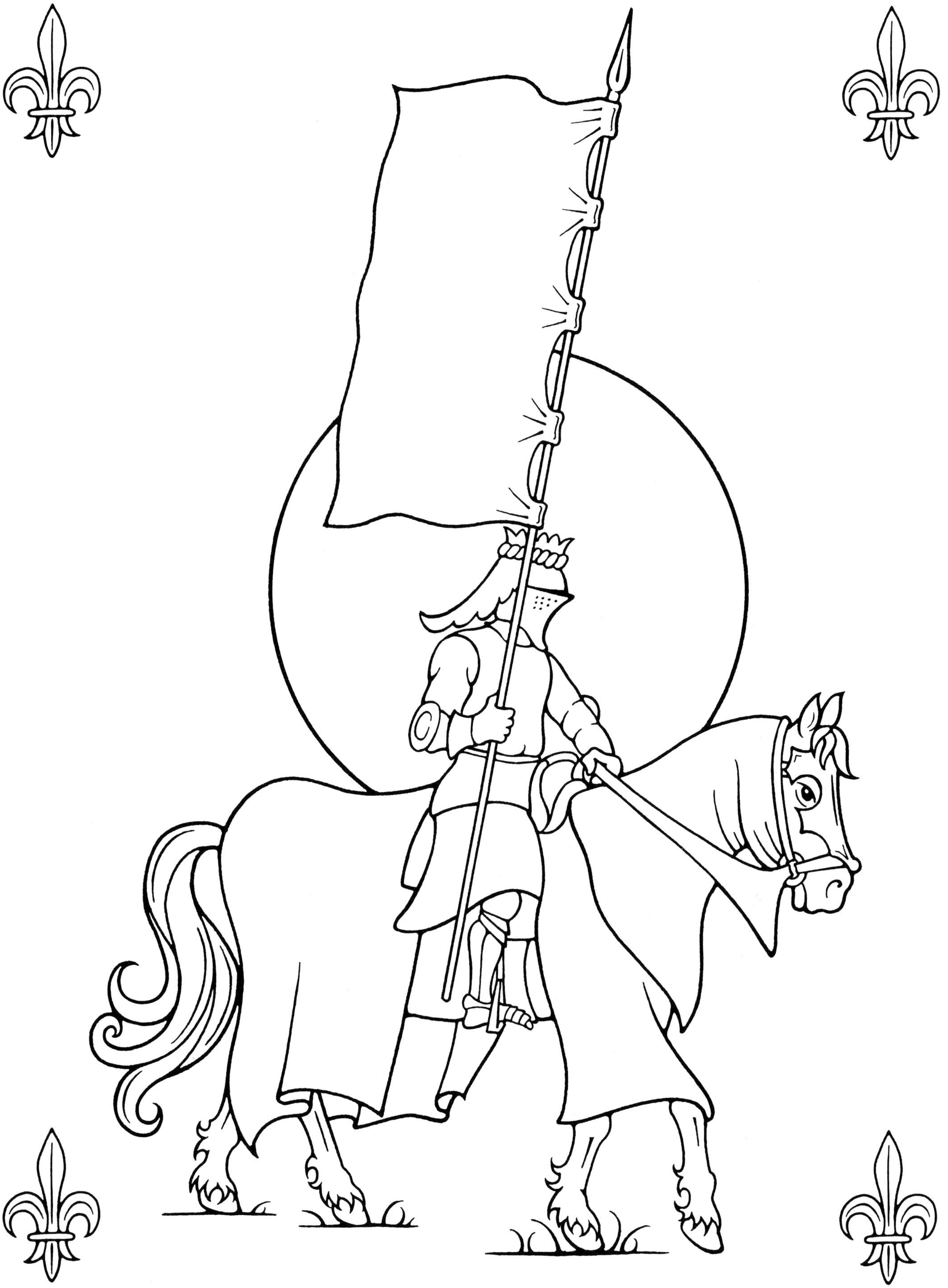

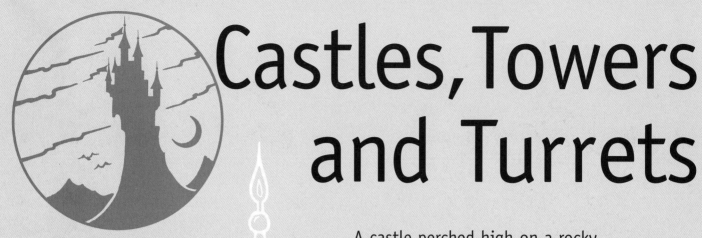

Castles, Towers and Turrets

A castle perched high on a rocky, impregnable outcrop, or a tottering tower, housing a wizard's spell room – these are places of strength and power to capture the imagination. The fantasy castle reflects the knowledge we have of castles through history, whilst relishing in the architectural impossiblities. Castles can be spooky or safe havens; in the world of fantasy they can be a home to heroes or the bolthole of villains.

The imagery in this section can be used to evoke the weird and unnatural, conjure up romantic scenes of far away and long ago, or simply suggest the fortresses of former times.

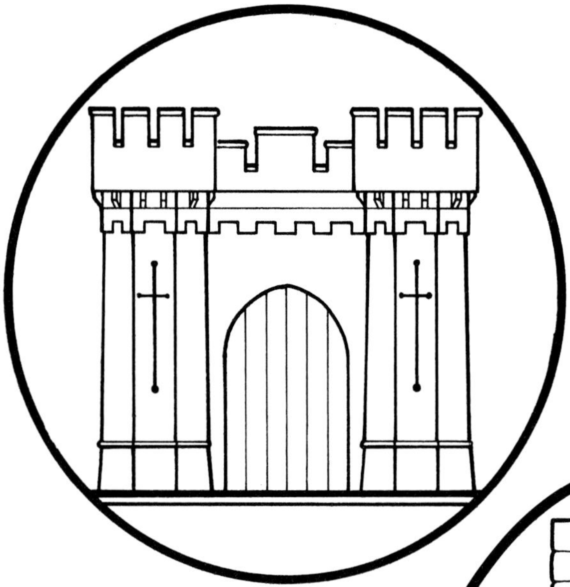

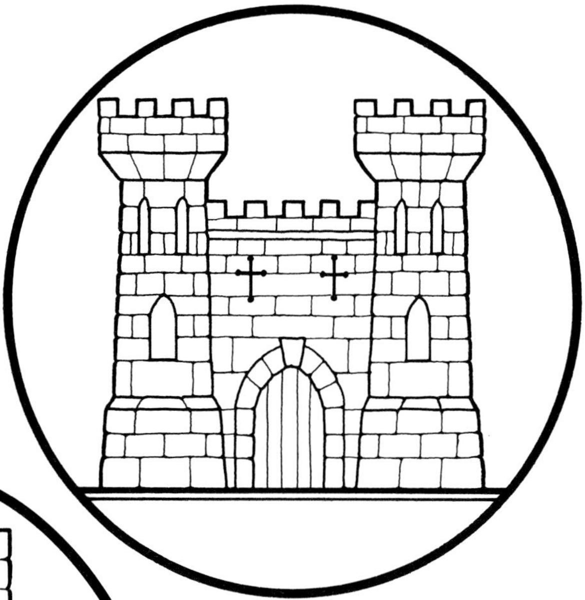

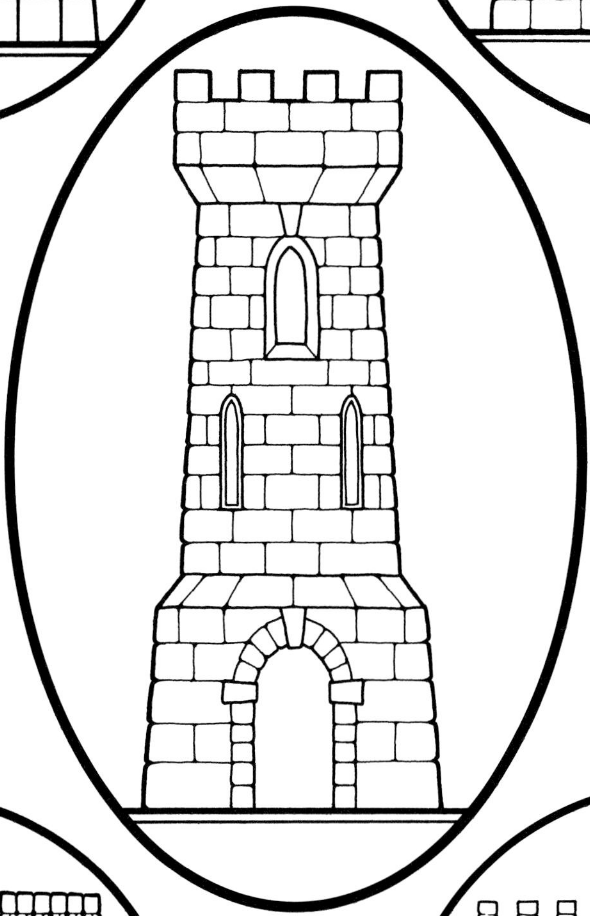

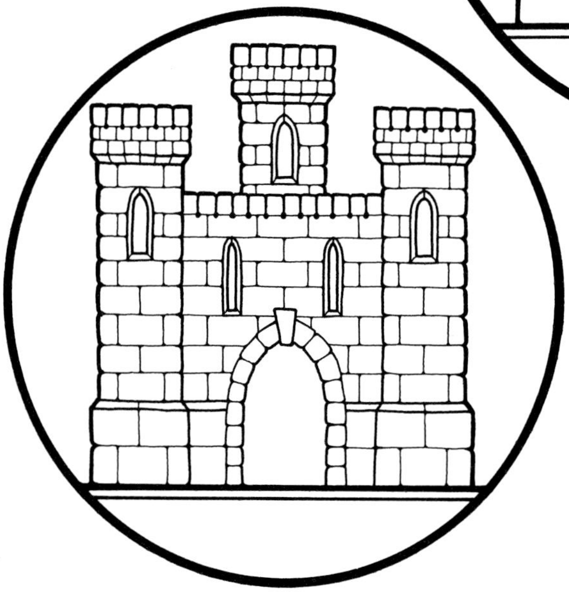

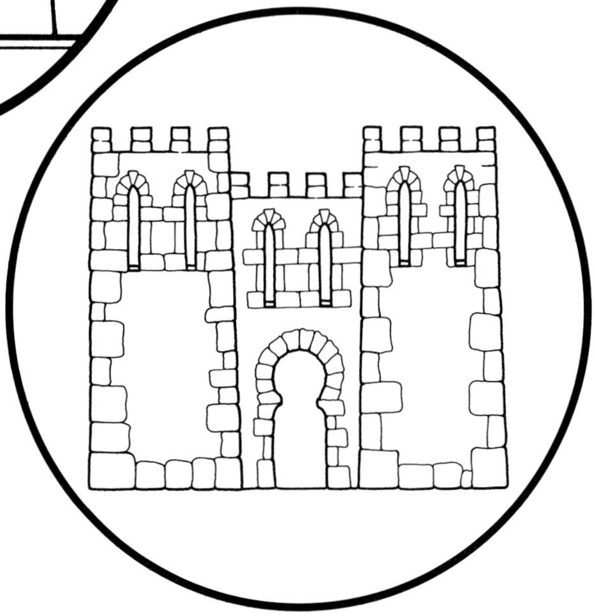

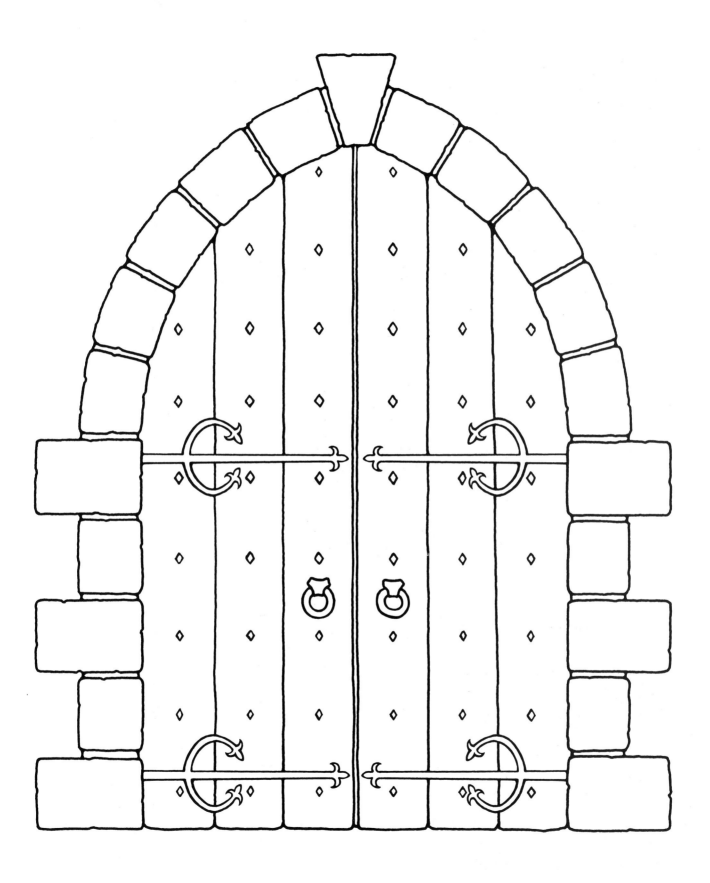

Other Worlds

Many stories are not just about characters but also the land that they inhabit. The landscape of the fantasy realm can reach back into our own history. Standing stones are testimony to our own past, although the mists of time obscure their origins and allow fantastical stories to grow up around them. In the legend of King Arthur and Camelot, the kingdom was said to flourish when the King did. Excalibur rising from the waters in the hand of the Lady of the Lake is a gift in order to enable king and land to prosper.

In the land of the imagination, there are many other worlds, and elements of those places may feature over the next few pages.

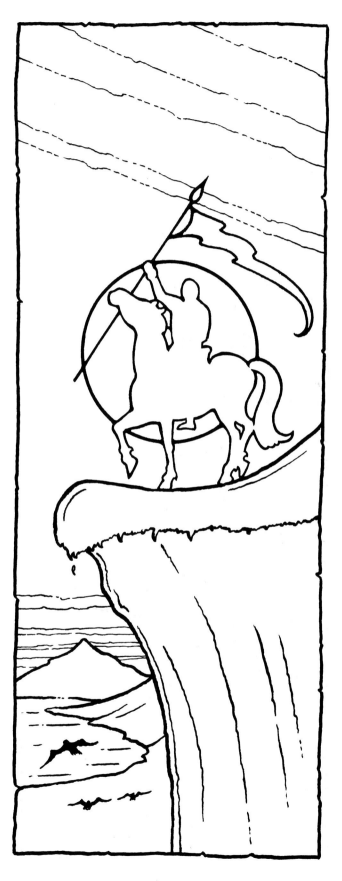

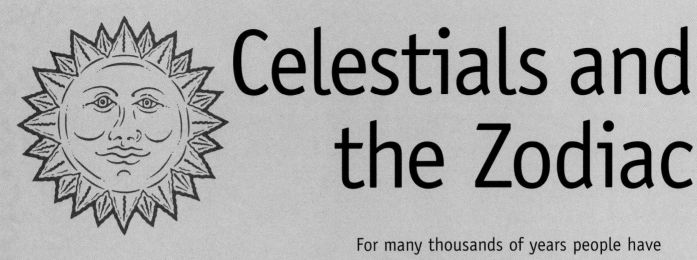

Celestials and the Zodiac

For many thousands of years people have been fascinated by the course of the sun, moon and stars. Ancient monuments, such as Stonehenge in southern England and some Mayan temples in central America, are now believed to have been erected to align with the sun and the moon. Ancient people worshipped these celestial bodies.

A belief that the movement of the heavenly bodies influences what is happening on earth is called astrology, and the position of the planets in relation to the earth and the stars at the time of a person's birth determines their horoscope sign. Many people have an interest in their horoscope, and the zodiac signs on the next few pages reflect this.

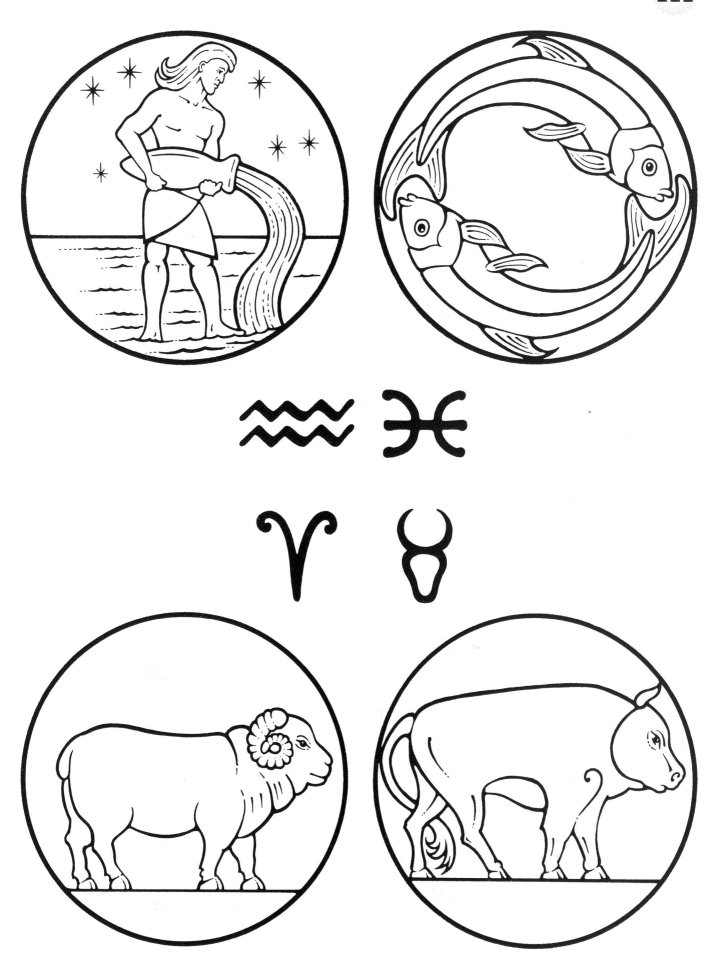

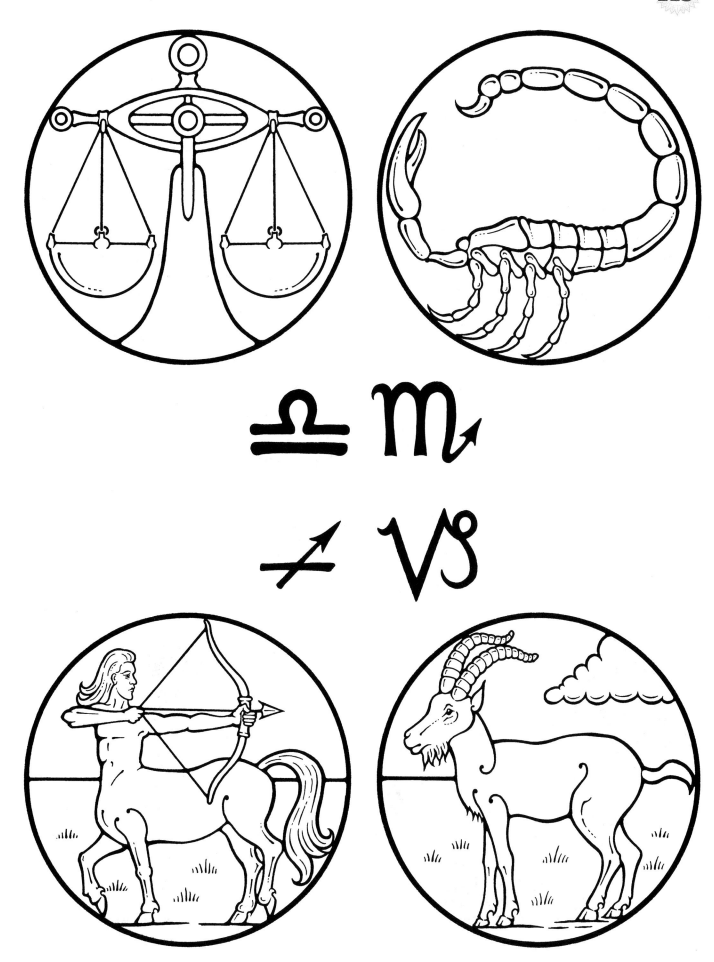

Borders and Backgrounds

A border or background can enhance a design, and here is a selection of circular, square and rectangular shapes that can be used to contain and emphasise any of the motifs in this book. A selection of patterns have been chosen to complement the themes of the motifs – leaves and flowers for the natural and fairy world; Celtic designs for witches and wizardry; and geometric patterns for knightly combats (although everything is open to interpretation).

Use these patterns as an inspiration – for instance, there are many different Celtic designs, and from the natural world you could draw upon shells, spirals and feathers to name just a few.

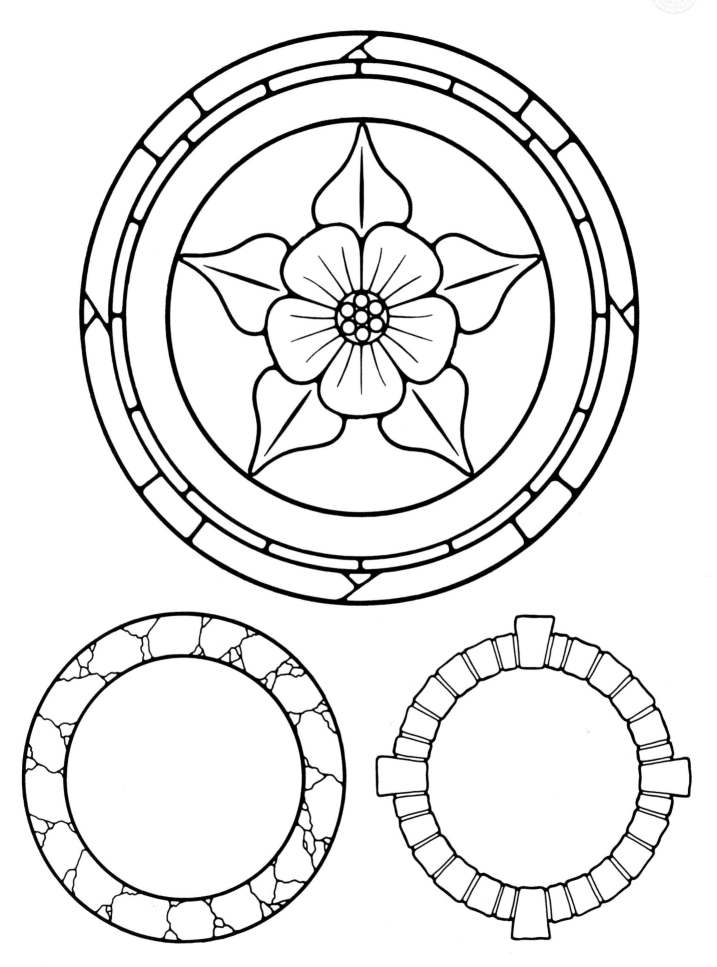

About the author

Chris Down was an architectural technician for eight years before becoming a freelance illustrator, specialising in Celtic art. His first set of Celtic cards was published in 1994. Since then, he has produced further art for cards, window transparencies, mugs, coasters, jewellery boxes and wall plaques. To date he has supplied illustrations for over thirty books, and this is his second book for David & Charles, in which he has turned his hand to fantasy art. His first book was Crafter's Design Library: Celtic. *Chris lives near Salisbury, England.*

Index